Origami Handbook
with English translation

Make Origami practical accessories

英訳付き

おりがみ
BOOK

Director of Ochanomizu Origami Kaikan
「お茶の水 おりがみ会館」館長
Kazuo Kobayashi 小林一夫

二見書房

gift

贈る人の気持ちが伝わるラッピング
Wrapping that communicates the giver's feeling

gift

kitchen

さりげない和の小物でおもてなしを
Provide hospitality with unassuming
Japanese accessories

kitchen

interior

レトロで美しい千代紙で華やかに！
Add a unique flair with beautifully retro chiyogami!

stationary

大人も楽しめる遊び心のある小物
Accessories with a whimsical gaiety for adults, too

event

季節の行事を大切に。祝日を美しく飾る
Honoring seasonal events: Beautifully decorate your holidays

CONTENTS

gift

ぽち袋 Pocchi Envelope	正方形のぽち袋 Square Pocchi Envelope	三角ギフトボックス Triangular Gift Box	プチギフトボックス Small Gift Box	バラのラッピングクリップ Rose Wrapping Clip
17	19	21	23	25

kitchen

鶏の箸置き Rooster Chopstick Stand	犬の箸置き Dog Chopstick Stand	カトラリーケース Cutlery Case	花の器 Small Flower Bowl	菓子鉢 Candy Bowl	鶴の器 Crane Bowl	コースター Coaster
27	29	31	33	35	37	39

はじめに Preface —————— 12
この本の使い方 Using this book —————— 13
きれいに折るコツ The Secret of Crisp Folds —————— 13
折り方の記号 Folding Symbols —————— 14
基本の折り方 Basic Folds —————— 16

kitchen

兜のボトルキャップ
Samurai Helmet
Bottle Cap

41

stationary

カードケース
Card Case

43

えんぴつのしおり
Pencil Bookmark

45

ハートの
メッセージカード
Heart Message Card

47

interior

フォトフレーム
Photo Frame

49

整理ボックス
Organizer Box

51

interior

鶴のメモスタンド
Crane Memo Stand

53

event

寿鶴
Crane of Longevity

55

内裏雛 めびな
Imperial Court Dolls
Empress

57

内裏雛 おびな
Imperial Court Dolls
Emperor

59

サンタのオーナメント
Santa Claus Ornament

61

靴下のオーナメント
Stocking Ornament

63

はじめに
Preface

　京都の公家社会からはじまって贅沢品だった千代紙は、その後、木版刷りの普及により庶民にも広がりました。そして、江戸文化のなかでさまざまな紋様が生まれ、伝承されてきたのです。千代紙の紋様には動物や植物、自然の風景や気象現象、暮らしの道具など、あらゆるモチーフが使われています。連続やつなぎ、あるいは散らすといったパターンも多彩で、デザインとしても美しく楽しめます。歌舞伎や舞踊などの文化に起源をもつものや縁起をかついだ吉祥紋様など、その由来を知ると、さらに千代紙の奥深さに触れることができるのではないでしょうか。

　色鮮やかな千代紙で、伝統的で身近な遊びである折り紙作品を作ってみませんか。本書では、実際に「使える小物」をコンセプトとして、24種類の折り方を紹介しています。見て美しい、折って使える千代紙の世界を楽しんでください。

小 林 一 夫

The chiyogami brightly colored paper with small designs of family crests, animals, plants, and natural phenomena that originated as a luxury item in Kyoto's court society later gained popularity among common people as use of wood block printing became widespread. Edo culture produced a wide variety of patterns handed down through the ages. Myriad motifs are used in chiyogami patterns that feature animals, plants, natural scenery, weather phenomena and the tools of everyday life. The array of serial, linking and spray patterns are in multiple colors that can also be appreciated for their beauty as designs. Some patterns have their origins in kabuki and Japanese dance cultures, while others are auspicious patterns that bear good fortune. Bolstered with an understanding of pattern origins, the reader can delve further into underpinnings of meaning in chiyogami.

I invite you to use to fold origami creations from festive chiyogami in a traditional pastime accessible to anyone, anywhere. This book instructs you in the folding techniques for twenty-four accessories designed for actual use. Immerse yourself in the world of chiyogami: appreciate the beauty of paper that can be folded into exquisite serviceable items.

Kazuo Kobayashi

この本の使い方
Using this book

- この本では、美しい千代紙を使って、24種類の「実際に使える小物」を折ることができます。

  This book guides you to create 24 varieties of accessories made from beautiful chiyogami that you can actually use.

- 折りたい作品を決めましょう。難易度を★の数で表わしているので、参考にしてください。

  Find a project that you want to make. The number of stars (★) expresses the origami project's level of difficulty.

  ★☆☆　とても簡単 Simple
  ★★☆　ふつう Intermediate
  ★★★　少し難しい Challenging

- ミシン目で千代紙をカットします。いちど折り目をつけてからカットすると、きれいに切れます。

  Cut the chiyogami on the perforation. Crease once before cutting to ensure a clean edge.

- p.65からの折り図を見ながら折ります。「折り方の記号」と「基本の折り方」は p.14〜16を参照してください。

  Look at the folding diagrams on page 65 as you make your project. For Folding Symbols and Basic Folds, please see pages 14–16.

- 折り上がった小物は、ぜひ暮らしのなかで使ってみてください。

  Use the origami accessories you create in your home.

ミシン目 — Perforation
作品名 — Project
作品の解説 — Description
折り方のページ — Folding Instructions Page

紋様の名前 — Pattern
紋様の解説 — Pattern Description
キリトリ線（切ってから折る場合） — Cut Line (for chiyogami that is cut prior to folding)

きれいに折るコツ　The Secret of Crisp Folds

・角と角をきちんと合わせて折りましょう。Align corners precisely before you fold.

・折り筋はしっかりとつけましょう。Flatten fold edges until sharp and crisp.

折り方の記号　Folding Symbols

線の種類や矢印など、この本で使う記号の説明をします。
記号は、折り図を見るときに必要になります。

This section describes types of lines, arrows and other symbols used in this book. You will need to understand these symbols when you view the Folding Diagrams.

紙の表と裏　Front and back of chiyogami paper

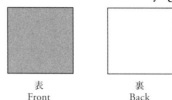

表
Front

裏
Back

谷折り　Valley fold

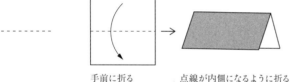

手前に折る
Fold towards yourself.

点線が内側になるように折る
Fold so that the dotted line is on the inside.

折り筋をつける　Make a crease

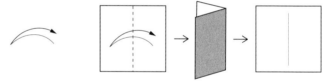

一度折って線をつけたあと、開いて元に戻す
Fold once to create a line in the paper and then unfold.

山折り　Mountain fold

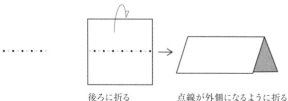

後ろに折る
Fold away from yourself.

点線が外側になるように折る
Fold so that the dotted line is on the outside.

矢印の方向に折る　Fold in the direction of the arrow

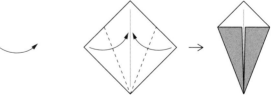

記号どおりに矢印方向に折る
Fold in the direction of the arrow as indicated by the symbol.

紙の向きを変える Change the position of the paper

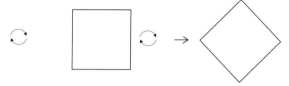

向きを変えたところ
New paper position.

紙の間を開く Open up the space created by a fold

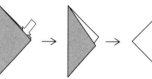

折った紙の間を開く
Open up the space between two or more layers of folded paper.

間を開いたところ
View of the space exposed by opening.

紙を裏返す Turn the paper over

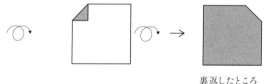

裏返したところ
View of the project after it is turned over.

ハサミで切る Cut with scissors

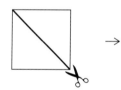

ハサミで切りこみを入れたり、切り落としたりする
Use scissors to make cuts and/or remove pieces of paper.

切ったところ
View after cutting.

図を拡大して示す Enlarge the diagram

拡大したところ
Enlarged view.

同じ幅 Same width

同じ角度 Same angle

基本の折り方 Basic Folds

複数の折り方に共通する、よく使う折り方の説明をします。
とくに「四角折り」と「中割り折り」はよく使います。

Let's learn several common folding techniques often used in origami. Of these, you will encounter the Square fold and Inside Reverse fold most frequently.

四角折り　Square fold

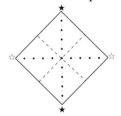

1
谷折り、山折りの折り筋をつける
Use the valley fold and mountain fold to crease the paper.

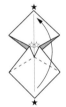

2
★と★、☆と☆がつくようにたたむ
Furl so that the ★ and ★ as well as the ☆ and ☆ touch at the tips.

3
できあがり
Finished!

中割り折り　Inside Reverse fold

1
まとめて折り筋をつけてから、谷折りは山折りに変える
First make all creases, and then change the valley folds to mountain folds.

2
先端を内側に入れるように折る
Fold so that the tip is tucked inside the paper.

3
できあがり
Finished!

段折り　Pleat fold

1
山折りと谷折りをする
Make a mountain fold and valley fold.

2
できあがり
Finished!

ぽち袋
Pocchi Envelope

子どものお年玉やちょっとしたお祝いなど、少額のお金を人に贈るときに使う小さな袋が「ぽち袋」です。関西弁の「これっぽっち」が語源となったもの。

A little envelope used to hold gifts of a small sum of money to congratulate someone, or that are given to children at New Year's is called a pocchi envelope. The Japanese name "pocchi-bukuro" comes from the Kansai dialect term "koreppocchi."

see page 65

三ツ面子守
みつめんこもり
Tri-Mask Babysitting

江戸時代には子守は少女の仕事であり、赤ん坊をおぶる姿がよく見られました。「三ツ面子守」は「恵比寿」「おかめ」「ひょっとこ」の面をかぶり替えながら、子守をする少女の踊り。3つの面を散らした楽しい柄です。

Babysitting was girls' work during the Edo period (1603- 1868), when girls carrying swaddled babies on their backs was a common sight. "Tri-Mask Babysitting" is a dance depicting young girls changing masks from the face of the god of wealth, to the humorous homely woman and ugly fellow to amuse their charges.

正方形のぽち袋
Square Pocchi Envelope

中心から全体を広げるように開く、「たとう折り」のぽち袋。開き口には千代紙の裏面が出て、縁取られるようになっています。正方形でかわいらしく、プレゼントにも！

Folded so that the entire envelope opens from its center, this square pocchi envelope is created using overlapping folding techniques. The back of the chiyogami shows at the opening, hinting to the bearer to grasp the edges. The cute square shape is an ideal gift!

see page 66

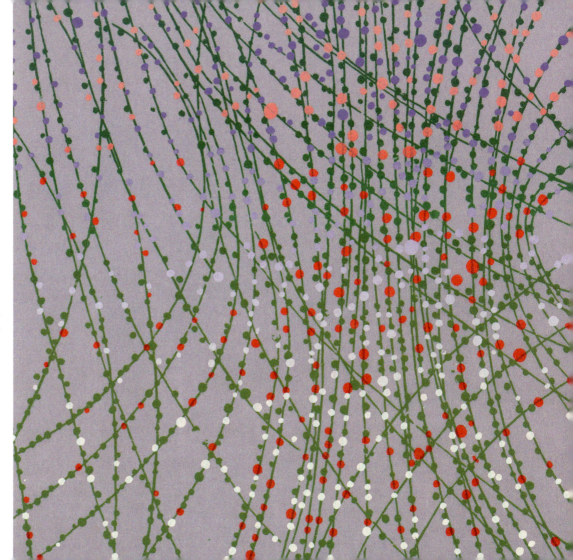

しだれ梅(うめ)
Shidare Ume (Drooping Plums)

梅は奈良時代に中国から渡り、『万葉集』にも多く詠まれるなど親しまれた花。ほかの花に先駆けて早春に咲くことから、縁起がいいともいわれます。しだれ梅は、美しい花とカーブした枝ぶりを楽しむ図案です。

The plum flowers so familiar to Japanese and regaled in the Man'youshuu came to Japan from China during the Nara period. Plums are said to be auspicious because they bloom earlier in spring than other flowers. The Drooping Plums design juxtaposes beautiful flowers with the graceful curves of bowing branches.

21

三角ギフトボックス
Triangular Gift Box

ピラミッド型のギフトボックスは、上部をシールなどでとめて使いましょう。千代紙の柄と色を合わせたマスキングテープを使うのもおすすめです。

Seal the top of this pyramid-shaped gift box with a sticker. You can also use masking tape to match the design and color of the chiyogami.

see page 67

小紋つづり
Fine Komon

一面に細かな柄をつけ、遠目には無地に見えるような紋様を「小紋」といいます。柄の種類や大きさが違う複数の小紋を、モザイクのようにつづって柄にしました。本来は地味に見える小紋が、華やかに生まれ変わっています。

Komon refers to a design of repeated fine patterns on one side of paper that appears as a solid color when viewed from a distance. Several komon of different types and pattern sizes are juxtaposed to create a larger mosaic design. The traditionally staid komon are reborn in this bright, gay design.

23

プチギフトボックス
Small Gift Box

1枚の紙だけで一体化したフタまで作れる、小さなギフトボックスです。指輪などのプレゼントを入れるのに最適。開けるときのわくわく感も贈れます。

This small gift box comes and its attached lid can be made with just one piece of paper. Perfect to a hold a ring or similar present, the box gifts the receiver with excitement at opening it as well as seeing what's inside.

see page 68

市松
Checkerboard

2色の正方形を交互に配置した格子紋様で、古くは桂離宮のふすまなどにも見られました。正式には「石畳紋様」ですが、江戸の歌舞伎役者、佐野川市松が衣装に使い大流行したため、「市松紋様」と呼ばれるようになりました。

A lattice pattern created by repeatedly alternating squares of two colors, the checkerboard pattern was used on sliding doors inside the Katsura Imperial Villa in Kyoto in ancient times. Formally known as the "paving stone pattern," the checkerboard pattern ("ichimatsu" in Japanese) took its current name when it became all the rage after Edo period kabuki actor Ichimatsu Sanogawa wore it on stage.

25

バラの
ラッピングクリップ
Rose Wrapping Clip

バラの花をラッピングの飾りにしましょう。花の中心と花弁のカールは、ピンセットではさんでクルクルとねじります。きつめにねじるのが、きれいな曲線を作るコツです。

Create this rose to crown a wrapped gift. Use a pin to secure the center of the flower and the petal edges as you twist. The tighter you twist, the more elegant the curves you create.

see page 70

あばれ青海
Turbulent Sea

半円で波紋様を表わす「青海波」に荒れ狂う波紋様を入れた「あばれ青海」。本来は青系の色が多かったものの、図案として広まるにつれ自由な色で使われるようになりました。千鳥や魚、動物との組み合わせも多く見られます。

The Turbulent Sea pattern depicts seigaiha, a wave design made of the arches of semicircles, interspersed with frothing waves. While blue hues were traditionally used more often, different colors were used freely as the design gained popularity. Plover, fish and animals are also often included in the design.

鶏の箸置き
Rooster Chopstick Stand

箸先をちょこんとのせられる箸置きが4つ作れます。十二支にも含まれる鶏は、昔からよく使われるモチーフ。顔と羽根を折る角度で鳥らしいフォルムが決まります。

You can make 4 chopstick stands to rest the tips of your chopsticks on. The rooster is a motif used since ancient times because the animal is included in the 12 signs of the Chinese zodiac. The angle of the face and wing folds give the stand its distinctly birdlike form.

see page 72

青海波
せいがいは
Seigaiha (Waves)

半円を規則的に繰り返し使った波紋様で、源氏物語の雅楽「青海波」の舞衣装として用いられた紋様です。同じ形を繰り返すことで吉事が繰り返され、一族の繁栄につながるとされる吉祥柄でもあります。

The regular repetition of semicircles in the seigaiha pattern was used on Imperial court dancer costumes in the Genji Monogatari (Tale of Genji). Repetition of the same shape is believed to spur ongoing good fortune in this auspicious design also thought to bring prosperity to the family clan.

犬の箸置き
Dog Chopstick Stand

長方形に切って、ダックスフンドのような胴長犬の箸置きが4つ作れます。胴部分の折り重ね方で全体の長さが決まります。割り箸の箸袋でも同じように作れます。

Origami paper is cut into rectangles to create 4 chopstick stands that resemble long-bodied Dachsunds. The layered folding technique of the dog torso determines the total body length. You can also use disposable chopstick wrappers to create these stands.

see page 73

毛まり
Kemari (Lion's Mane)

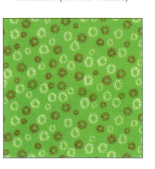

正月に厄払いのために家々をまわる縁起ものの獅子舞は、緑色に赤、白の毛まり紋様の布をかぶっています。獅子の毛が丸まった状態を図案化したもので「獅子毛」とも呼ばれ、江戸のおめでたい定番柄のひとつです。

Dancers of the Lion Dance believed to foster good luck performed at people's homes in the New Year to exorcise evil spirits. They wore cloths of red and white lion's mane kemari patterns on a forest green background. This circular design of hair from a lion's mane is also called the Lion's Mane pattern, and was a classic celebratory patterns of the Edo period.

31

カトラリーケース
Cutlery Case

和菓子に使う黒文字や、小さなデザートスプーンなどが入るカトラリーケース。お茶菓子を楽しむひとときに、千代紙の小物で和のあしらいをそえましょう。

This cutlery case is a sheath for the toothpick utensil used to eat Japanese confections or a small Western dessert spoon. Accent your table with a touch of Japanese ambiance from this chiyogami accessory.

see page 74

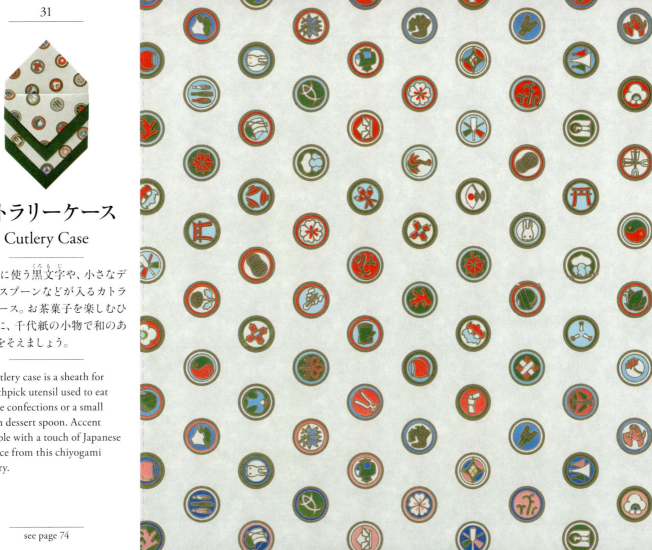

道 成 寺
Doujouji (Doujouji Temple)

歌舞伎役者の家を表わす家紋も、着物や千代紙の定番紋様となっています。「道成寺」を踊るときの帯に家紋がデザインされたように、千代紙にさまざまな家紋を遊び心いっぱいに集めました。

Family crests that represent family clans of kabuki actors are also classic patterns for kimonos and chiyogami. A variety of family crests are playfully collected on chiyogami in the same way that family crest designs decorated the obi belts of kabuki dancers performing the Doujouji dance.

花の器
Small Flower Bowl

小鉢のようにきれいに花弁が開いた、花の形の器です。カラフルな千代紙で作り、菓子などを入れて置くだけで、テーブルの上が明るく華やぎます。

Pretty, blooming flower petals form a flower-shaped vessel like a Japanese kobachi dish. Made from colorful chiyogami, simply placing the small flower bowl on the table with candy or other small items inside brightens and lends gaiety to a room.

see page 75

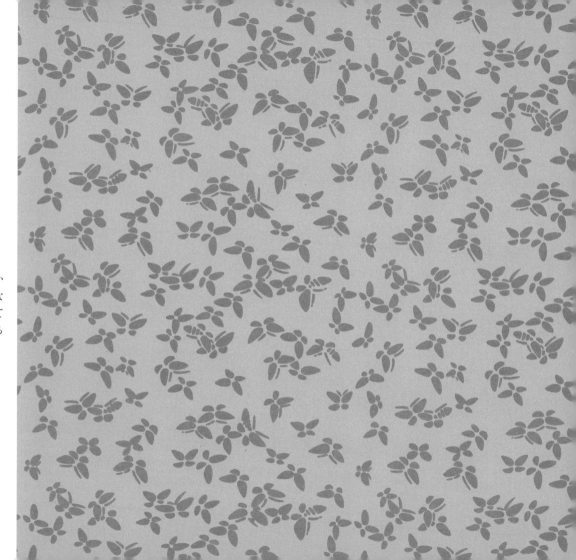

蝶
Butterfly

蝶は中国から伝わり、古くは鎌倉時代から紋様に使われました。青虫からさなぎになり羽化するさまが再生や命のよみがえりを意味するとされ、縁起のいい紋様です。武家では不死不滅への願いを込めて用いられました。

Butterflies come to Japan from China and were used as patterns as far back in history as the Kamakura era (1185-1333). The caterpillar's transformation into a chrysallis and then a winged creature is thought to symbolize rebirth and renewed life in this auspicious pattern. Warrior class family clans used the pattern to pray for immortality of the family line.

35

菓子鉢
Candy Bowl

古くから伝承されている折り紙で、ちょっとした菓子を入れるのにぴったりです。ひな祭りのあられや、小さな金平糖や豆菓子など、見た目も楽しく使えます。

Perfect for holding a small confection, this origami has been passed down since ancient times. Whether it's arare rice biscuits for Doll's Festival or small kompeito sugar candy and bean cakes, this bowl adds a whimsical air to whatever it contains.

see page 76

鳥獣戯画
Choju Giga
(Bird and Beast Caricature)

京都の高山寺に伝わる絵巻物「鳥獣戯画」は、世界最古の漫画とされる国宝です。ウサギやカエル、サルを擬人化した有名な甲巻を、江戸の洒落をきかせて千代紙に写しました。楽しい世界観を味わってください。

The Choju Giga picture scrolls housed in Kyoto's Kozanji Temple is a national treasure believed to be the world's oldest comic book. Glimpse Edo-era (1608-1868) humor in the fantastical worldview of anthropomorphic rabbits, frogs and monkeys from a renowned ancient] scroll reproduced on chiyogami for you to enjoy.

鶴の器
Crane Bowl

折り紙の定番アイテム「鶴」を、小さな器に。日本では丹頂鶴は神の使いとされ、信仰の対象にもなっていました。鶴は和の小物に欠かせないモチーフなのです。

The classic origami crane made into a small bowl. The Japanese red-crowned crane is said to a messenger of the gods and was itself an object of religious belief. The crane is an indispensable motif in Japanese accessories.

see page 78

雲立涌
Hourglass Clouds

曲線が縦に走る連続紋様は、水蒸気がゆらゆらと上るさまをデザイン化した「立涌」という紋様。雲立涌は有職紋様のひとつとして身分の高い公家の装束に用いられ、後々には能装束にも使われるようになりました。

The continuous pattern of vertical curvilinear lines create a pattern called tatewaku, designed to evoke the image of langorously rising steam. Hourglass clouds were one of the patterns used in the garments of the high nobility that were later also adopted for use in Noh plays.

コースター
Coaster

1枚の和紙を折ってものを包むことを「たとう折り」といいます。このコースターはたとう折りのアレンジで、きれいな折り紋様に仕上げています。

Folding one sheet of washi paper to fully envelop something without using any tape or fastener is called tatou-ori. The arrangement of tatou-ori folds create a finish of cleanly folded patterns.

see page 80

吉原つなぎ
Yoshiwara Links

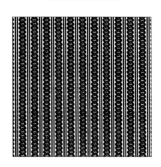

吉原の茶屋ののれん柄が由来となり、茶屋で働く男衆の着物の柄としても広まりました。四角形の角をくぼませて縦に連続させたことで「つなぎ」と呼ばれます。内側に細い線を入れたこのタイプは「子持ち吉原」です。

Originating in the noren split curtain of tea houses in Yoshiwara, this pattern was used widely on the kimonos of servants who worked in tea houses. The pattern is called "links" for the repetition of vertically linked quadrangles. This version with a thin line on the inside of the quadrangle is "Mother Yoshiwara."

41

かぶと
兜のボトルキャップ
Samurai Helmet Bottle Cap

武士が防具とした甲冑の兜は、男の子の成長を願って節句に飾る縁起ものです。簡単に作れる折り紙の定番で、大きな紙で作れば子どもがかぶることもできます。

The samurai helmet warriors used as armor is an auspicious decoration displayed during the Boys' Festival that expresses the hope of growth and good health for boys. A classic origami project that is simple to make, the Samurai Helmet Bottle Cap can be made using a large piece of paper to enable a child to actually wear it.

see page 82

歌舞伎
Kabuki

江戸歌舞伎には役者紋、定番の衣装など、さまざまな紋様が意味を持って使われています。紗綾形、水、七宝、松、波など、歌舞伎でもおなじみの柄を、帯状にデザインした千代紙です。

A multitude of patterns on actor's crests and classic costumes are used to convey meaning in Edo kabuki. This chiyogami is decorated with wide bands of familiar kabuki patterns such as a pattern of interlocking swastikas, water, the seven treasures, pine and waves.

43

カードケース
Card Case

名刺やカードを入れられるシンプルなケースです。きっちりと薄く折って作り、手帳などに入れて使うのもおすすめです。

A simple case that can hold business cards or credit cards. Create using sharp, thin creases and put the case inside your planner so it's ready to use.

see page 84

菱松
Diamond Pine

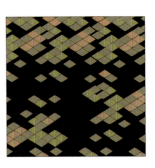

「菱形」は沼地に群生する菱という水草の実の形から名づけられました。古くは正倉院の宝物に使われ、植物を菱形にした紋様も多く見られます。菱形の松を散らした「はなれ菱松」を千代紙にしました。

The term "diamond" shape refers the shape of seeds from aquatic plant Trapa japonica (similar to a water caltrop) that grows in colonies in marshes. In ancient times, Trapa japonica was housed in the Shoso-in treasure house of Todai-ji temple, prompting many patterns of plants drawn in this diamond shape. This chiyogami depicts diamond-shaped pine scattered over the surface in a "separated diamond pine" pattern.

えんぴつのしおり
Pencil Bookmark

千代紙を長方形に3つに切って作るしおりです。鉛筆の外側と芯の部分に、千代紙の紋様が出ます。本や手帳にはさむと便利です。

Chiyogami is cut lengthwise into three strips to make this bookmark. The chiyogami pattern appears on the pencil exterior and the lead point. Create something useful to mark your place in a book or planner.

縞
(しま)
Stripes

縞は江戸時代の着物に大流行した柄です。もともと染めるのが簡単で庶民にも広まったという背景もありますが、太さを変えたり曲線を混ぜたりと、バリエーションの多さからも当時の人気がうかがえます。

Stripes were tremendously popular as a kimono pattern during the Edo period. Reasons are that it was popular with commoners because it was always easy to dye, but its popularity at the time is also attributable to the number of variations possible by changing stripe thickness or adding curved lines.

ハートの メッセージカード
Heart Message Card

裏面の罫線部分にメッセージを書いて折りましょう。最後の折り返しをそのまま使えばダイヤ、曲線に切ればハートになります。パーティの招待状などにもいいですね。

Write a message to the recipient of this project on the lined back of the chiyogami before you fold. Use the last turnup fold as-is to make a tire, or cut it into a curve to make a heart. This card is suitable for a party invitation or similar message.

see page 86

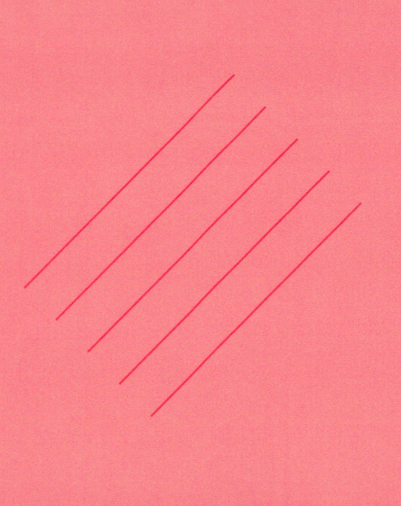

48

大柄藤
おおがらふじ
Large Wisteria

房状に花咲く藤は豪華で美しく、藤原家にまつわる紋様としても知られています。上下に入れるばかりでなく、左右やランダムに配置されたものなど種類は豊富。花の中に「ふ」の字を入れる粋な図案も人気です。

Wisteria blooms goregeous flowers in a tufted bunch and is a pattern recognized to honor the Fujiwara family clan. Plentiful varieties of this pattern include not only flowers positioned at the top and bottom, but also at random to the left and right. Chic patterns in which the Japanese hiragana "fu" is written in the wisteria ("fuji" in Japanese) are also popular.

フォトフレーム
Photo Frame

四方から折りこんでいくだけで、簡単にフレームが作れます。一度折ってみてから、飾りたい写真のサイズを確認して、開き部分より大きめにカットしましょう。

Easily make a photo frame by simply folding from each of the four directions. Fold the frame once to ensure the size of the photograph you want to frame will fit, and then cut the opening slightly larger than the photo size.

see page 87

バラ
Roses

昔よりバラの自生地であった日本に「花の女王」として広く知られたのは、明治時代のウィーン博覧会の頃と考えられます。千代紙のバラは大正時代にデザインされ、木版画で刷られたもの。大正ロマンをいまに伝える千代紙です。

Japan was a natural habitat for roses since ancient times, but the flower only became known in Japan as the Queen of Flowers around the time of the Vienna World Exposition during the Meiji era (1868-1912). Rose chiyogami was designed and engraved on wood block prints during the Taisho era (1912-1926). This chiyogami conveys the atmosphere of the Taisho Roman movment even today.

整理ボックス
Organizer Box

シンプルな正方形の箱は伝承の形です。同じサイズで2つ折ると、片方をフタにしてぴったりと組めます。紙を5mmずつ小さくしてたくさん作れば、入れ子の箱もできます。

The simple square-shaped box is a traditioal shape. Fold the paper into two sections of identical size with one section as the perfectly fitting lid. Use sheets of paper that are each 5 mm smaller than the last to create a series of nested boxes that fit one inside the other.

ことぶき鶴
Crane of Long Life

鶴は長寿の象徴として、またよいことの前兆を示す吉祥として、数多く使われています。常緑で風雪に耐えることからやはり長寿とされる松と合わせて、はばたく鶴を配置した縁起のよい図案です。

Cranes are prevalent symbols of longevity or as lucky omens that portent good fortune. This auspicious pattern combines a crane in flight with the evergreen pine, symbolizing longevity for its ability to withstand wind and storm.

鶴のメモスタンド
Crane Memo Stand

ちょっとしたメモなどをはさんで置くことができる、鶴の形のメモスタンドです。手作りの和の小物で、デスクまわりを楽しく飾りましょう。

This is a stand in the shape of a crane that can hold small notes or memos. A hand-made Japanese accessory to accent your desk.

see page 89

矢羽
Arrow Feathers

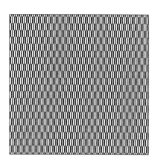

弓矢は「魔をはらう」とされ、おもに女性の着物に用いられる定番の紋様となっていました。江戸時代には大奥の下級女中が着ていたり、明治・大正時代には女学生にも流行したものです。

Arrows were believed to exorcise evil and were a classic pattern used mainly on women's kimonos. Lesser courtiers of maidservants in O-oku wore it during the Edo period, while the pattern flourished among female students during the Meiji and Taisho periods.

ことぶきつる
寿 鶴
Crane of Longevity

長寿につながる縁起物の鶴は、正月飾りとしておすすめです。金色の千代紙で扇のように羽根を広げた鶴を折れば、金屏風のよう。よりいっそうおめでたい雰囲気が演出できます。

The auspicious crane linked to a long life is recommended for use as a New Year's decoration. Folding a crane with wings outstretched like a fan from gold chiyogami is reminiscent of a gold-leafed folding screen. Decorating with the Crane of Longevity origami heightens the sense of celebration to any occasion.

see page 90

四ツ花菱(よつはなびし)
Four Flower Diamond Crest

四弁の花を菱形(ひしがた)にデザインした花菱を4つ組み合わせています。花菱は平安時代以来、公家の装束などにも用いられたもので、伝統と格式のある有職紋様(ゆうそく)のひとつ。さまざまなタイプの菱形の組み合わせがあります。

Four groups of flowers are combined in a diamond shape design. Flower diamonds are one type of traditional crest used on court noble attire since the Heian era (794-1185) to indicate a person's social standing. Many types of diamond crest combinations exist.

内裏雛・めびな
Imperial Court Dolls Empress

内裏雛は、3月3日の桃の節句に女児の成長を願って飾られます。平安時代に無病息災を願って神に祈り、紙やワラなどの人形(ひとがた)を川に流した厄払いが起源とされます。

Dolls depicting the Emperor and Empress are displayed as decorations on Girls' Day in Japan. In the Heian era (794-1185), the dolls were a form of prayer to the gods for good health, and are believed to have their origins in the paper and straw dolls that people released in rivers to drive away evil spirits as they floated away.

see page 92

牡丹蝶
Peony Butterfly

よみがえりにつながる吉祥紋様の蝶は、ひらひらと舞う華やかな姿でも人気です。左右対称の鮮やかな揚羽蝶を、花や葉、川や水の流れなどと組ませた紋様も豊富。「花の王」といわれる牡丹と蝶は、その代表的なものです。

The butterfly, an auspicious symbol linked to rebirth, is well-liked for the way it lightly flutters as though dancing through the air. Many designs combine the bright swallowtail butterfly with flowers, leaves, rivers or running water. The peony, called the King of Flowers, depicted with the butterfly is one representative pattern.

内裏雛・おびな
Imperial Court Dolls
Emperor

「内裏」とは天皇のお住まいである御所のことなので、元来、おびなとめびなは天皇、皇后の姿をあらわしています。

Since the "dairi" refers to the Imperial Palace where the Emperor and Empress of Japan live, the imperial court dolls of the Emperor and Empress basically refer to the personages of the Emporer and Empress themselves.

see page 92

花菱立涌
はなびしたてわく
Hourglass of Diamond Flowers

曲線がふくらんで縦につらなる連続紋様「立涌」の中に、花菱をあしらった紋様です。立涌は奈良時代から使われており、内側に植物やほかの紋様を配したさまざまなパターンが見られる優美な紋様として知られています。

This pattern features diamond flowers encapsulated by curved lines that alternately flare and narrow in a lengthwise hourglass pattern. Used since the Nara period, the variety of patterns of animals and other designs depicted inside the hourglass lines make the Hourglass of Diamond Flowers an exquisite pattern.

サンタの オーナメント
Santa Claus Ornament

クリスマス飾りも和の千代紙で作ると、ひと味ちがった雰囲気が楽しめます。ひもをつけてクリスマスツリーに飾ったり、シンプルに壁に貼るのもよいでしょう。

Using Japanese chiyogami to make your Christmas decorations lends a touch of uniquemenss to the look you create. Attach a string to this project to hang it from your Christmas tree or simply hang on the wall.

see page 94

扇面小紋
Fine Fan Pattern

扇は広げた形が末広がりになることから、繁栄につながる吉祥紋様とされています。開いた扇の扇面に、とても細かな小紋を入れこんだ図案。千代紙や着物には、動植物だけでなくこうした小紋柄も多いのです。

Since the shape of an open fan spreads out, the fan is an auspicious symbol of increasing prosperity. This design features finely detailed patterns on the the surface of an open fan. Many chiyogami and kimonos have fine patterns like these as well as animals and plants on them.

靴下の
オーナメント
Stocking Ornament

雪の結晶を模した「雪花(せっか)」の紋様は、オーナメントにおすすめです。簡単に作れる千代紙のオーナメントで、クリスマスを楽しく飾りましょう。

The Snowflake pattern made from snow crystals is wonderful for use on ornaments. Make decorating for Christmas enjoyable with easy to make chiyogami ornaments.

see page 95

雪花
Snowflakes

雲や波、月、星など、自然の風景や現象も紋様となっています。雪の結晶をデザインした雪花紋様は、江戸時代後期に流行したもの。美しい結晶を描いた『雪華図説』という紋様集まで出版されました。

Clouds, waves, the moon, starts and other natural scenes and phenomena are also used in patterns. The Snowflake pattern designed with snow crystals was popular in the second half of the Edo period. So popular were these beautiful crystals that a collection of patterns was published in a book entitled, "Illustrated Snowflakes."

ぽち袋 Pocchi Envelope　難易度 Difficulty ★★★

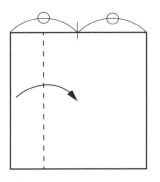

1

紙の半分に合うように谷折り

Make a valley fold so that one edge aligns with the paper center.

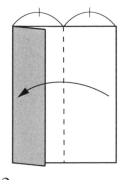

2

残り半分で谷折り

Make another valley fold with the remaining half of the paper.

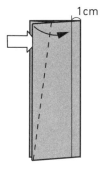

3

上の1枚を斜めに谷折り

Fold the top layer in a diagonal valley fold as shown.

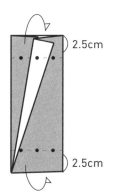

4

図の位置で上下を山折り

Make mountain folds at the positions shown at the top and bottom of the envelope.

5

できあがり

Finished!

see page 17

正方形のぽち袋 Square Pocchi Envelope　　難易度 Difficulty ★☆☆

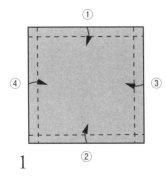

1

①②③④の順に、端を少し谷折り

Make narrow valley folds in order at edges ①, ②, ③ and ④.

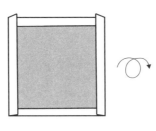

2

折ったところ

Folded view.

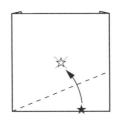

3

中心(☆)に印をつけ、★と☆を合わせて谷折り

Mark the center (shown here with a ☆) and align the ★ and ☆ to make a valley fold.

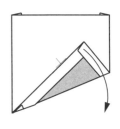

4

3で折ったところを元に戻す。残り3ヶ所も同様に折り筋をつける

Unfold the flap you folded in Step 3. Make creases the same way on the remaining 3 sides.

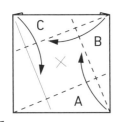

5

ABCの順に、折り筋どおりに谷折り

Make valley folds in order on the A, B and C creases.

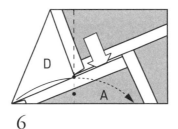

6

Dを折り筋どおりにたたみながら、Aの中に入れる

Tuck D into A as you fold on the crease.

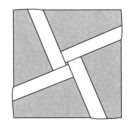

7

できあがり

Finished!

see page 19

三角ギフトボックス Triangular Gift Box　難易度 Difficulty ★★☆

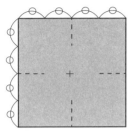

1
中心に印をつけ、図の位置に折り筋をつける

Make a mark in the center and creases in the positions shown.

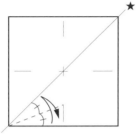

2
★の補助線に合わせて折り筋をつける。残り7ヶ所も同様に折り筋をつける

Make a crease along the guide line marked by ★. Do the same in the remaining 7 locations.

3
折り筋をつけたところ

View with creases.

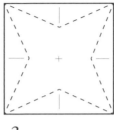

4
折り筋が交わる点を結んで、谷折りの折り筋をつける

Make a crease to create a square that connects the points where the last creases intersect.

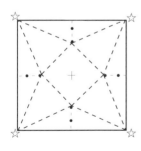

5
折り筋どおりに折りたたみ、4つの☆を合わせる

Fold along creases so that the 4 tips marked by ☆s meet.

6
折りたたんでいるところ

View during folding.

7
できあがり。ギフトを入れたら、開かないようにシールやマスキングテープなどでとめる

The finished project is shown at left. Enclose a gift, and seal with a sticker or masking tape so that the gift box does not come open.

see page 21

プチギフトボックス　Small Gift Box　難易度 Difficulty ★★★

原案：ジョバンニ・マルタリアータ

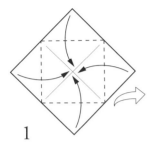

1
三角に折り筋をつけてから、角を中心に合わせて折る
Make creases in a triangular shape and fold the corners into the center.

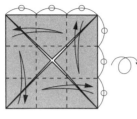

2
1/3のところで折り筋をつける
Make creases to divide each side into thirds.

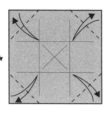

3
図の位置に折り筋をつける
Make the creases at the positions shown.

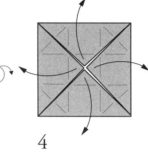

4
折ったところをすべて開く
Open all the folds you made.

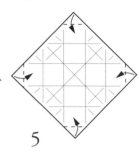

5
角をすべて谷折り
Make valley folds at all corners.

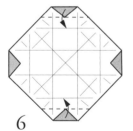

6
上下を谷折り
Make valley folds at the top and bottom.

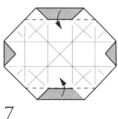

7
さらに上下を谷折り
Make another set of valley folds at the top and bottom.

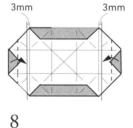

8
左右を、図の折り筋から3㎜外側に合わせて谷折り
Make valley folds at a point 3 mm outside the creases in the diagram.

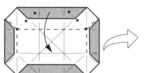

9
図のように折り筋を付け直して、折りたたむ
Re-crease again as shown in the diagram and fold the top side.

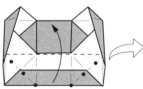

10
もう片側も同様に折りたたむ
Fold the other side in the same way as Step 9.

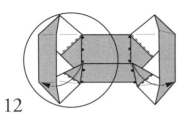

12

上下を開いて立ち上げる。図のように折り筋をつけて、左右を立ち上げ、折り筋どおりに折って押しこむ

Spread apart the edges of the paper at the top and bottom. Make creases as shown in the diagram, and spread apart the right and left sides of the box to make them three-dimensional. Then fold along the creases, tucking paper inward to form the side of a box.

13

折りたたんでいるところ

Close-up of folding along creases and tucking paper inward to form a side.

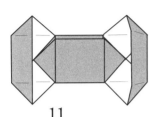

11

折りたたんだところ

View after folding.

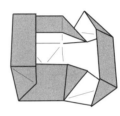

14

左側を折りたたんだところ。右側も同じに

View of the folded left side. Fold the right side in the same way.

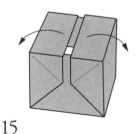

15

両方を折りたたんだら、外側の箱をいちど開く

When both sides are folded, open the outer box.

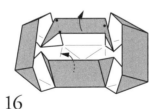

16

内側の箱の中へ折りこんである部分を持ち上げ、箱の上部を形作る

Lift the parts tucked inside the box interior to create the shape of the box's top half.

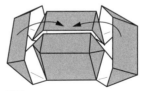

17

内側の箱ができたら、外側の箱を折りたたんで閉じる

When the inner box is complete, refold the outer box to close.

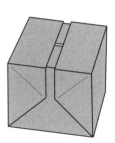

18

できあがり
Finished!

see page 23

バラのラッピングクリップ　Rose Wrapping Clip　難易度 Difficulty ★★★

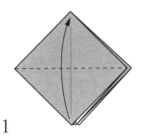

1

「四角折り」から始め、上の1枚を
谷折り。裏も同じに

Start with a square fold and fold
the top layer into a valley fold. Do
the same on the reverse side.

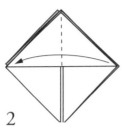

2

上の1組を左に折る。
裏も同じに

Fold the top set of layers
to the left. Do the same
on the reverse side.

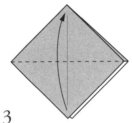

3

上の1枚を谷折り。裏も同じに

Make the top layer into a
valley fold. Do the same on
the reverse side.

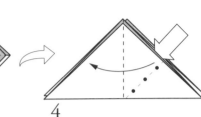

4

右の1組の間を開いて折りたたむ

Open up the space between 1 set
of layers on the right and fold.

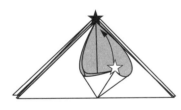

5

左側2枚、右側1枚で間を開き、4の折り筋
どおりに折りたたんで☆を★に合わせる

Open up the 2 sets on the left side and
1 set on the right side. Fold on the four
creases, matching the tips ☆ to ★.

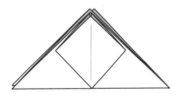

6

折りたたんだところ。
残りの3ヶ所も同じに

One side is now folded. Do the
same on the remaining 3 sides.

7

中心(8の★)をつまみ、
まわりの花びら部分を開く

Pinch the center (the 8 ★ s) closed,
and pull out the petals around it.

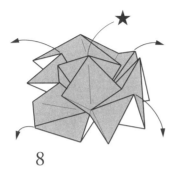

8

開いているところ

View of the open rose.

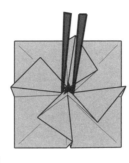

9

中心★をピンセットではさみ、
時計回りに2〜3回きつくねじる

Secure the center ★ with tweezers and tightly rotate the chiyogami clockwise 2 – 3 times.

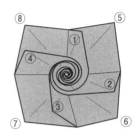

10

まわりを少し開く。①〜⑧の8つの角が花びらになる

Slightly tug petals open further. The eight corners labelled ① – ⑧ become rose petals.

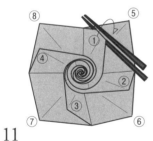

11

①から順に、ピンセットで角を外側にカールさせる

Use tweezers to curl the corners outward in numerical order.

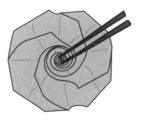

12

最後にもう一度中心をきつくねじって、形を整える

Lastly, twist the center tightly one more time to perfect your rose's shape.

13

できあがり

Finished!

see page 25

鶏の箸置き　Rooster Chopstick Stand

難易度 Difficulty ★☆☆

※紙を点線で4つに切って作る
Cut paper on the dotted line to make 4 pieces.

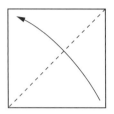

1

半分の三角に谷折り

Make a valley fold to create a triangle half the paper size.

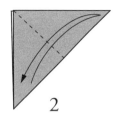

2

折り筋をつける

Crease as shown.

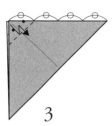

3

上の1枚を「段折り」

Make a pleat fold in the top layer.

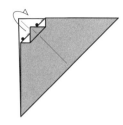

4

下の1枚を、上の1枚の谷折り線に合わせて山折り

Make a mountain fold on the bottom layer in the location shown.

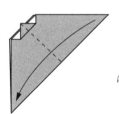

5

全体を半分に谷折り

Fold the entire project in half in a valley fold.

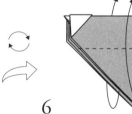

6

羽根部分を上に向けて谷折り。裏も同じに

Position the wings upward and make a valley fold. Do the same on the reverse side.

7

トサカ部分を上に引き上げ、右下の角を内側に山折り。裏も同じに

Pull the bird's crest upward and make a mountain fold of the lower right corner towards the inside of the bird. Do the same on the reverse side.

8

できあがり

Finished!

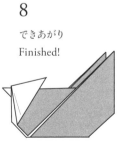

see page 27

犬の箸置き Dog Chopstick Stand

難易度 Difficulty ★★☆

※紙を点線で4つに切って作る
Cut paper on the dotted line to make 4 pieces.

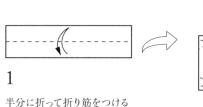

1
半分に折って折り筋をつける
Fold in half and crease.

2
右から順に図のように折る
Fold in order from the right as shown in the diagram.

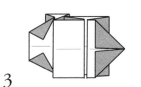

3
折ったところ。2のAのみ開く
Folded view. Open 2-A only.

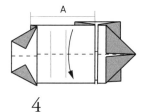

4
半分に折る
Fold in half.

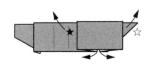

5
★と☆を上に引き上げる
Pull the ★ and ☆ upwards.

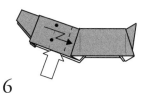

6
間を開き、折り筋どおりにかぶせるように「段折り」
Open up the space indicated by the arrow and make a pleat fold along the creases as though covering them with a hat.

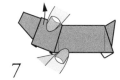

7
頭部を引き上げる
Pull up the dog's head.

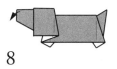

8
鼻先をつまんで下げる
Pinch the tip of the snout and pull downward.

9
できあがり
Finished!

see page 29

カトラリーケース Cutlery Case   難易度 Difficulty ★★☆

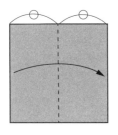

1

半分に谷折り
Fold in half in a valley fold.

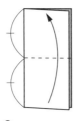

2

半分に谷折り
Fold in half in a valley fold.

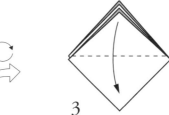

3

上の1枚を谷折り
Fold the top layer in a valley fold.

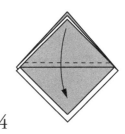

4

上の1枚を少しずらして谷折り
Realign the top layer slightly and make a valley fold.

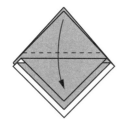

5

さらに上の1枚を少しずらして谷折り
Realign the next top layer slightly and make a valley fold again.

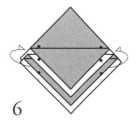

6

左右を山折り
Make mountain folds on the left and right sides.

7

できあがり
Finished!

see page 31

花の器 Small Flower Bowl　難易度 Difficulty ★★★

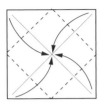

1

三角に折り筋をつけてから、角を中心に合わせて折る

Make creases in a triangular pattern, and then align the corners to the center and fold.

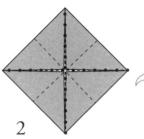

2

折り筋をつけて「四角折り」

Make creases and then make the square fold.

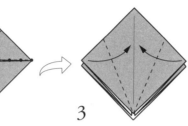

3

上の1枚を真ん中に合わせ谷折り。裏も同じに

Align the top layer with the center and make a valley fold. Do the same on the reverse side.

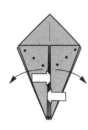

4

図のように折り筋をつけてから、間を開いてたたむ。裏も同じに

Make creases as shown in the diagram, and then open each section and fold on the creases. Do the same on the reverse side.

5

たたんだところ

View after folding

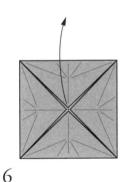

6

2の形に戻して、1ヶ所開く

Unfold to the shape shown in Step 2 and then open one of the triangles.

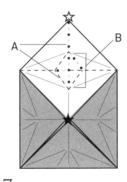

7

折り筋をつけ直し、A、Bの順に折りたたむ

Re-crease, and then fold A and B in order.

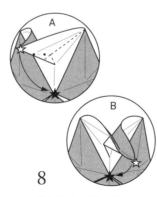

8

たたんでいるところ

View during folding.

9

1ヶ所折りたたんだところ。残り3ヶ所も同じに

View with one triangle folded. Fold the remaining 3 in the same way.

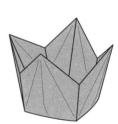

10

できあがり

Finished!

see page 33

菓子鉢 Candy Bowl　難易度 Difficulty ★★☆

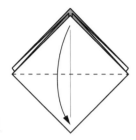

1

表を上にして「四角折り」し、上の1枚を谷折り。裏も同じに

Hold the paper with the front side facing you and make a square fold. Then fold the top layer in a valley fold. Do the same on the reverse side.

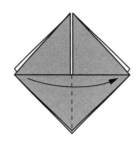

2

上の1組を右に折る。裏も同じに

Fold the top set of layers to the right. Do the same on the reverse side.

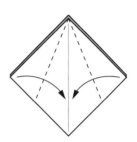

3

左右とも上の1枚を谷折り。裏も同じに

Fold the top layer on both the left and right in a valley fold. Do the same on the reverse side.

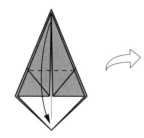

4

上の1枚を谷折り。裏も同じに

Fold the top layer in a valley fold. Do the same on the reverse side.

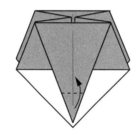

5

図のように谷折り。裏も同じに

Make a valley fold as shown in the diagram. Do the same on the reverse side.

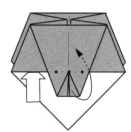

6

間を開いて山折りで差し入れる。裏も同じに

Open up the sections you just folded, and make a mountain fold and tuck it under the open area. Do the same on the reverse side.

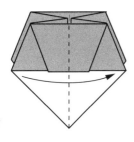

7

上の1組を右に折る。裏も同じに

Fold the top set of layers to the right. Do the same on the reverse side.

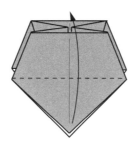

8

上の1枚を点線のところで上に折る。裏も同じに

Fold the top layer upward on the dotted line. Do the same on the reverse side.

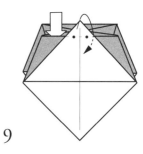

9

飛び出た角を内側に折りこむ。裏も同じに

Tuck protruding corners inside. Do the same on the reverse side.

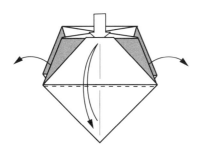

10

まとめて折り筋をつけてから、上から 間を開いて底を広げ、形を整える

First make all creases, and then open up the spaces beginning at the top (indicated by the arrow). Widen the base and perfect the shape of your candy bowl.

11

できあがり

Finished!

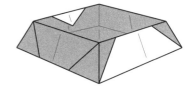

鶴の器 Crane Bowl　難易度 Difficulty ★★★

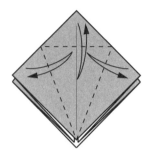

1
「四角折り」から始め、図のように折り筋をつける
Start with a square fold, and make creases as shown in the diagram.

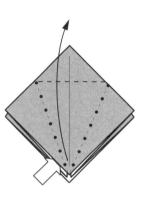

2
上の1枚を開いて折りたたむ
Open up the top layer and fold as shown.

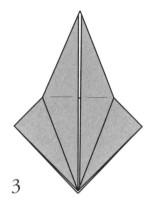

3
折りたたんだところ。裏も同じに
The folded project. The reverse side looks the same.

4
表を上にして全部開く
With the front facing you, open up all sections.

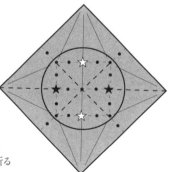

5
図のように折り筋をつけ直し、★と★、☆と☆が合うように折る
Re-crease as shown in the diagram, and fold by matching ★ with ★ and ☆ with ☆.

6
折りたたんでいるところ。中央をくぼませて折る
View of the bowl as you fold. Fold so that a hollow space is left in the center.

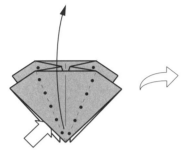 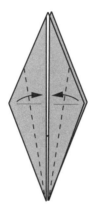 

7
間を開き、折り筋どおりに折りたたむ。
裏も同じに

Open up the section indicated by the arrow, and fold along the creases. Do the same on the reverse side.

8
真ん中に合わせて折る。
裏も同じに

Fold so that the corners meet at the center as shown. Do the same on the reverse side.

9
左右を「中割り折り」

Make inside reverse folds on the left and the right.

  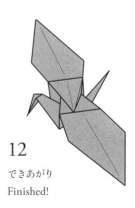

10
「中割り折り」で頭部を作る

Use an inside reverse fold to create the head.

11
羽根を開いて折る。裏も同じに

Open the wings and fold downward. Do the same on the reverse side.

12
できあがり
Finished!

see page 37

コースター Coaster　難易度 Difficulty ★★☆

原案：渡部浩美

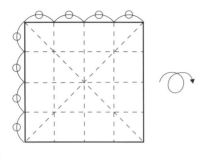

1

図のように折り筋をつける
Make creases as shown in the diagram.

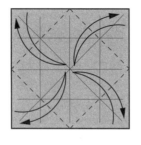

2

中心に向かって折り、戻す
Fold towards the center and then unfold.

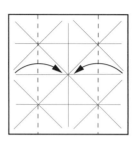

3

中心線に合わせて谷折り
Make valley folds so that both sides meet at the center.

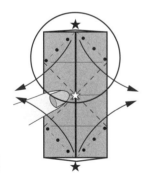

4

☆をおさえて、★と☆が合うように折りたたむ
Hold down the ☆, and fold as you open up the top layers on the left and right so that the ★ and ☆ meet.

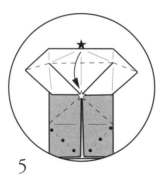

5

折りたたんでいるところ
View during folding.

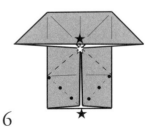

6

上部を折りたたんだところ。
反対側（手前）も同様に折りたたむ
View of a folded top half. Fold the opposite side (facing you) in the same way.

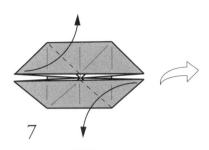

7

図のように谷折り
Make valley folds as shown in the diagram.

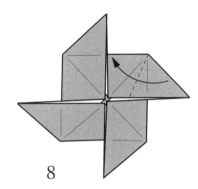

8

上端に合わせて谷折り
Make a valley fold that aligns with the top edge.

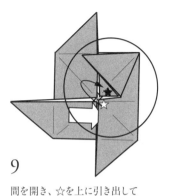

9

間を開き、☆を上に引き出して★の上にのせる
Open up that section, and pull the ☆ upward to cover the top of the ★.

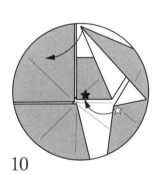

10

☆を★の上にのせるところ
View while placing the ☆ on top of the ★.

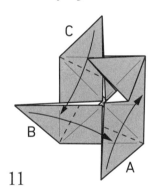

11

ABCの順に、残り3ヶ所も同様に折る
Fold the remaining 3 locations in order in the same way.

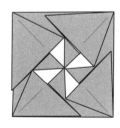

12

できあがり
Finished!

see page 39

兜のボトルキャップ Samurai Helmet Bottle Cap   難易度 Difficulty ★★☆

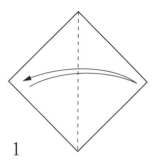

1

半分に折って折り筋をつける
Fold in half to crease.

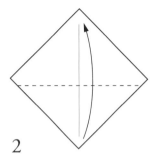

2

上を少しあけて谷折り
Leaving a little extra room in the top half, make a valley fold.

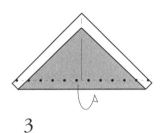

3

下を山折り
Make a mountain fold of the bottom.

4

☆と★がつくように谷折り
Make a valley fold so that the two ☆ s meet the ★.

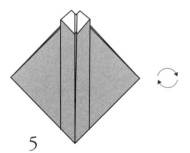

5

折ったところ
Folded view.

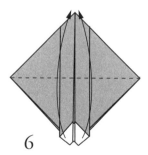

6

上の1枚を半分に谷折り
Fold the top layer in half in a valley fold.

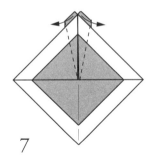

7

図のように斜めに谷折り
Make a diagonal valley fold as shown in the diagram.

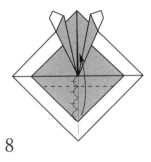

8
上の1枚を1/4のところで谷折り
Make valley folds that divide the top layer into quarters.

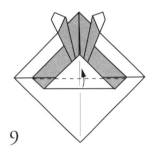

9
図のように上の2枚を折り上げる
Fold the top two layers upward as shown.

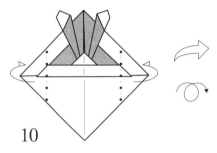

10
左右を裏へ折り返す
Fold the left and right sides to the back.

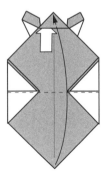

11
半分に折り、
間を開いて三角の中へ差しこむ
Fold in half, open up the space created, and tuck the corner inside the triangle marked by the arrow.

12
差しこんだところ
View with corner tucked in.

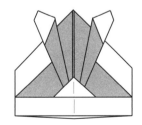

13
できあがり
Finished!

see page 41

カードケース　Card Case　難易度 Difficulty ★☆☆

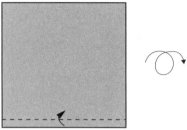

1

下を少し谷折り
Fold a small part of the bottom into a valley fold.

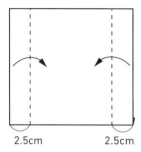

2

左右から2.5cmで谷折り
Make valley folds at 2.5cm from the left and the right.

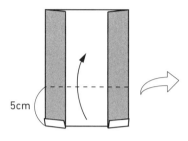

3

下から5cmで谷折り
Make a valley fold 5cm from the bottom.

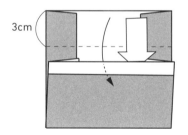

4

上から3cmで谷折りし、間を開いて差しこむ
Make a valley fold 3 cm from the top. Open up the bottom section and tuck in the top flap.

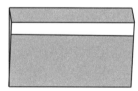

5

できあがり
Finished!

see page 43

えんぴつのしおり Pencil Bookmark

難易度 Difficulty ★★★

※紙を点線で3つに切って作る
Cut paper on the dotted line to make 3 pieces.

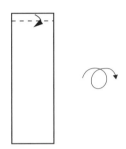

1

上を少し谷折り
Fold a small part of the top in a valley fold.

2

真ん中に合わせて角を折る
Fold corners so that they meet in the center.

3

もういちど真ん中に合わせて折る
Fold corners again so that they meet in the center.

4

折ったところ
Folded view.

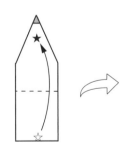

5

☆が★につくように谷折り
Make a valley fold so that the ☆ touches the ★.

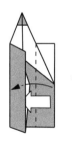

6

左右を図の位置で山折り
Make mountain folds on the left and the right at the positions shown.

7

左側の間を開き、右側を差しこむ
Open up the left side and tuck it into the right side.

表 Front　裏 Back

8

できあがり
Finished!

see page 45

ハートのメッセージカード Heart Message Card

難易度 Difficulty ★★★

原案：細谷純子

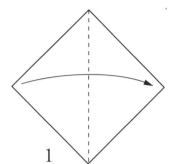

1
三角に谷折り
Make a valley fold to create triangles.

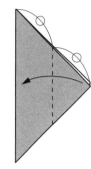

2
中心に向かって2枚いっしょに谷折り
Fold two layers together in a valley fold towards the center of the paper.

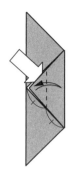

3
上の1枚を半分で折って、折り筋をつける
Fold the top layer in half and make a crease.

4
2枚いっしょに図のように切る
Cut two layers together as shown in the diagram.

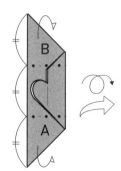

5
上下をA、Bの順で山折り
Make mountain folds in the top and bottom in A and B order.

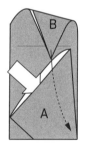

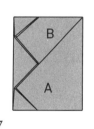

6
Aの間を開いてBを差しこむ
Open up the space created in section A and tuck B into it.

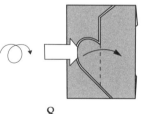

7
差しこんだところ
View of B tucked into A.

8
上の1枚を谷折りで開く
Make a valley fold in the top layer and open up the space created (see arrow).

9
できあがり
Finished!

see page 47

フォトフレーム Photo Frame

難易度 Difficulty ★★★

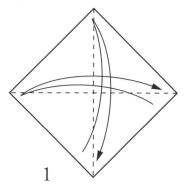

1

折り筋をつける
Make creases as shown.

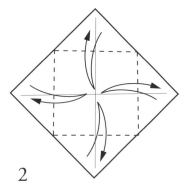

2

4つの角を中心に合わせ、
折り筋をつける
Align the four corners with the
center of the paper and make creases.

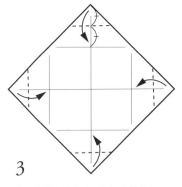

3

角から折り筋までの1/2で谷折り
Make valley folds halfway from each
corner to the nearest crease as shown.

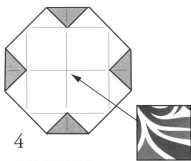

4

中心に写真を貼る
Affix a photo in the center.

see page 49

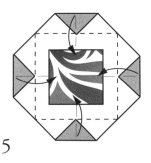

5

谷折りし、フレームが開かないように
貼りつける
Make a valley fold and secure so
that the frame does not come open.

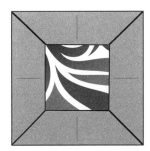

6

できあがり
Finished!

整理ボックス　Organizer Box

難易度 Difficulty ★★☆

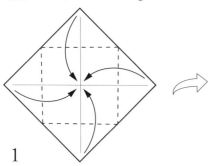

1
三角に折り筋をつけてから、角を中心に合わせて折る

Make creases to form triangles and then fold the corners so that they all meet in the center.

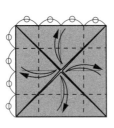

2
図のように折り筋をつける

Crease as shown in the diagram.

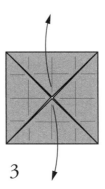

3
上下を開く

Open the top and bottom.

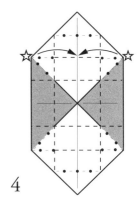

4
図のように折り筋をつけ直し、☆と☆を合わせて立ち上げる

Re-crease as shown, and spread open the edges so that both ☆ s meet in the center.

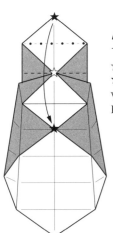

5
☆を合わせたところ。★と★を合わせて折りたたむ

View of ☆ s touching in the center. Fold so that the two ★ s meet.

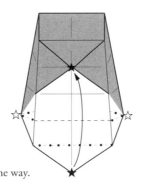

6
反対側（手前）も同様に折りたたむ

Fold the opposite side (facing you) in the same way.

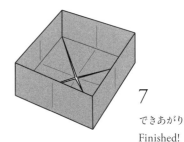

7
できあがり
Finished!

see page 51

鶴のメモスタンド Crane Memo Stand

難易度 Difficulty ★★☆

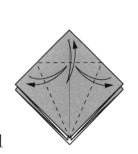

1

「四角折り」から始め、図のように折り筋をつける

Start with the square fold and crease as shown in the diagram.

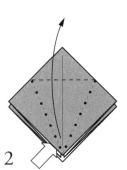

2

上の1枚を開いて折りたたむ

Open up the section under the top layer and fold.

3

折りたたんだところ。裏も同じに

View after folding. Do the same on the reverse side.

4

上の1組を左に折る。裏も同じに

Fold the top set of layers to the left. Do the same on the reverse side.

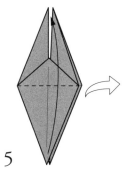

5

上の1枚を折り上げる。裏も同じに

Fold up the top layer. Do the same on the reverse side.

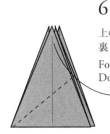

6

上の1枚を斜めに折る。裏も同じに

Fold the top layer diagonally. Do the same on the reverse side.

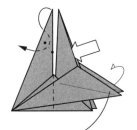

7

左側を「中割り折り」して頭を作る。羽根を点線で谷折りし、尾を平らに開く

Make an inside reverse fold on the left side to create the head. Make a valley fold on the dotted lines of the wings and flatten the tail open.

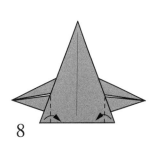

8

後ろから見た図。左右の端を折る

Diagram of the rear view. Fold the left and right tips as shown.

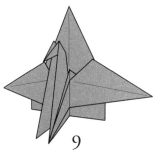

9

できあがり

Finished!

see page 53

寿鶴 Crane of Longevity　難易度 Difficulty ★★☆

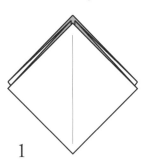

1

表を上にして「四角折り」
Make a square fold with the front facing you.

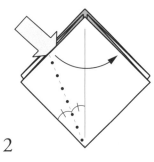

2

折り筋をつけてから、間を開いてつぶす
Make creases, open up the spaces created (see arrow) and then flatten.

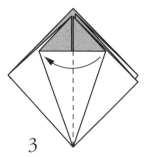

3

上の1枚を左に折る
Fold the top layer to the left.

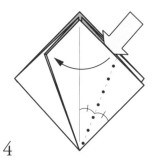

4

右側も同様に、折り筋をつけてから間を開いてつぶし、上の1枚を右に折る
Do the same on the right side: make creases, open up the spaces created (see arrow) and then fold the top layer to the right.

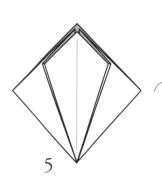

5

折ったところ
Folded view.

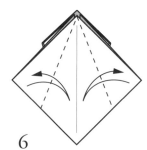

6

図のように折り筋をつける
Make creases as shown in the diagram.

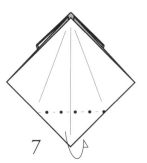

7

下を山折りする
Fold the bottom in a mountain fold.

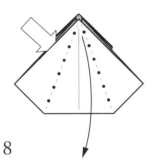

8

折り筋どおりに開いてたたむ

Open up spaces indicated by the arrow and fold along creases.

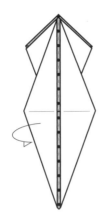

9

全体を半分に山折りする

Fold the entire project in half in a mountain fold.

10

折り筋をつけ、右下部の間を開いて、折り筋どおりにかぶせるように折る

Make a crease and then open up the spaces created in the lower right indicated by the arrow. Fold along the crease as though covering it with a hat.

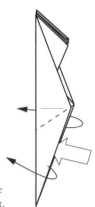

11

折り筋をつけて「中割り折り」

Make creases and then make an inside reverse fold.

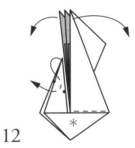

12

「中割り折り」で頭を作り、＊を押さえて羽根を広げる

Create the head using an inside reverse fold, and hold down the sections marked with ＊ as you spread the wings.

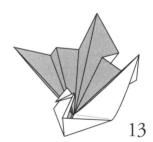

13

できあがり

Finished!

see page 55

内裏雛 めびな・おびな Imperial Court Dolls Emperor and Empress

難易度 Difficulty ★★★

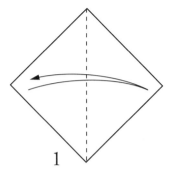

1
折り筋をつける
Make a crease.

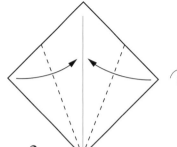

2
折り筋に合わせて谷折り
Make valley folds along the creases.

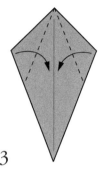

3
折り筋に合わせて谷折り
Make valley folds along the creases.

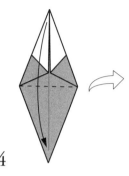

4
全体を半分に谷折り
Fold the entire project in half in a valley fold.

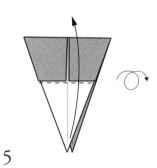

5
上の1枚を図の位置で谷折り
Fold the top layer in a valley fold at the position shown.

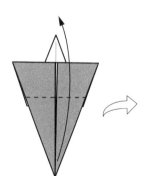

6
上の1枚を図の位置で谷折り
Fold the top layer in a valley fold at the position shown.

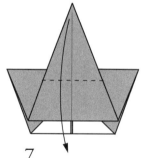

7
図の位置で谷折り
Make a valley fold on the dotted line shown.

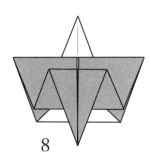

8
折ったところ
Folded view.

※折り方は8まで共通
The folding techniques up to Step 8 are the same for both dolls.

【めびな】
Empress

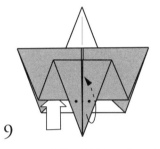 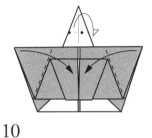 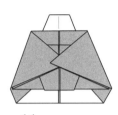

9

間を開き、先端を山折りして差しこむ
Open up the space created, make a mountain folds in the tip and tuck it into the space indicated by the arrow.

10

左右の角を谷折りし、頭を山折り
Make valley folds in the right and left corners and a mountain fold in the head.

11

めびなのできあがり
Finished Empress!

【おびな】
Emperor

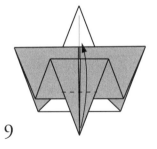 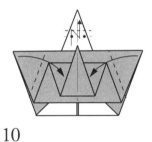 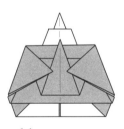

9

図の位置で谷折り
Make a valley fold as shown.

10

左右の角を谷折りし、頭を「段折り」
Make valley folds in the right and left corners, and make a pleat fold in the head.

11

おびなのできあがり
Finished Emperor!

see page 57, 59

サンタのオーナメント Santa Claus Ornament　難易度 Difficulty ★☆☆

原案：中島進

1

下を少し谷折り
Fold a small part of the bottom into a valley fold.

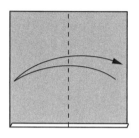

2

半分のところで折り筋をつける
Make a crease that divides the paper in half.

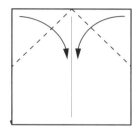

3

折り筋に合わせて谷折り
Make valley folds along the creases.

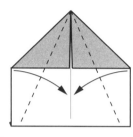

4

もう一度折り筋に合わせて谷折り
Make two more valley folds along the creases.

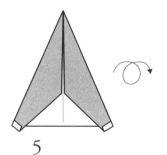

5

折ったところ
Folded view.

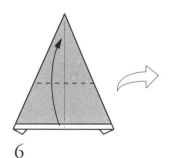

6

下から谷折り
Fold the bottom upwards to make a valley fold.

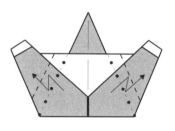

7

「段折り」して腕を作る
Make a pleat fold to create the arms.

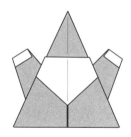

8

できあがり
Finished!

see page 61

靴下のオーナメント　Stocking Ornament

難易度 Difficulty ★★☆

1

図の位置で山折り

Make a mountain fold at the position shown.

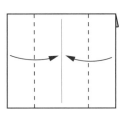

2

半分に折って折り筋をつけ、折り筋に合わせて左右を谷折り

Fold the chiyogami in half to crease, and then make valley folds on the left and right along the creases.

3

折ったところ

Folded view.

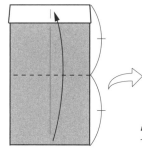

4

全体を半分に折る

Fold the entire project in half as shown.

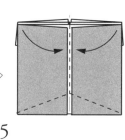

5

上の1枚を図のように谷折り

Make a valley fold in the top layer as shown in the diagram.

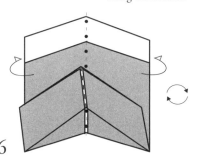

6

全体を半分に山折り

Fold the entire project in half in a mountain fold.

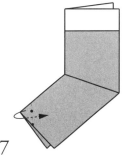

7

図の位置で「中割り折り」

Make an inside reverse fold at the position shown.

8

上の1枚を山折り。裏も同じに

Make a mountain fold in the top layer. Do the same on the reverse side.

9

できあがり

Finished!

see page 63

小林一夫

1941年、東京・湯島に生まれる。東京にある「お茶の水 おりがみ会館」館長。安政5年(1858年)創業の和紙の老舗「ゆしまの小林」4代目、社長。NPO法人国際おりがみ協会理事長。折り紙の展示や、教室の開催、講演などを通じ、和紙文化の普及と継承に力を注いでいる。折り紙を本格的に折り始めたのは30代から。特に先人の知恵や技を感じることのできる伝承の折り紙を愛し、古くから日本人の心に根ざし、生活の中にある折り紙のあり方を伝播させている。

その活動場所は日本のみならず世界各国に及び、日本文化の紹介、国際交流にもつとめている。近著に『折り、願い、遊ぶ―折紙の文化史』(里文出版)、『英語・仏語・中国語訳付き 鶴のおりがみBOOK』(二見書房)、『折り紙は泣いている』(愛育社)、『はじめての実用おりがみ』(朝日新聞出版)など。その他監修も多数手がけている。

Kazuo Kobayashi

Born in Yushima, Tokyo, in 1941, Kazuo Kobayashi is a director of Ochanomizu Origami Kaikan,Tokyo,and the fourth president of renowned washi store Yushima no Kobayashi(est. 1858). He also spreads and pass on washi culture and traditions by holding exhibitions, seminars and lectures as a director of the International Origami Association, an NPO corporation. He began seriously creating his own origami works in his thirties. Kobayashi's deepest passion is passing on origami traditions that feature the wisdom and unique skill of the ancients, and propagate the role of origami in everyday life rooted in the hearts and minds of the Japanese people for centuries. Active not only in Japan, Kobayashi travels worldwide to showcase Japanese culture and promote international exchange. Recent publishing of his books include Cultural History of Origami(Ribun Publications),Origami wa Naiteiru (Origami is Crying) (published by Aiikusha), and First Practical Origami(Asahi Shimbun Publications Inc.). Kobayashi has also acted as a supervising editor for many publications about Origami.

英訳付き おりがみBOOK

著者	小林一夫
発行	株式会社 二見書房
	東京都千代田区神田三崎町2-18-11
	電話 03(3515)2311［営業］
	03(3515)2313［編集］
	振替 00170-4-2639
印刷・製本	株式会社堀内印刷所

作品制作	渡部浩美
折り図作成	岩田ワレス奈穂子
デザイン	ヤマシタツトム
撮影	寺岡みゆき
スタイリング・執筆協力	宮野明子
翻訳	トライベクトル株式会社
編集協力	河英実（おりがみ会館）
千代紙協力	お茶の水 おりがみ会館

落丁・乱丁がありましたら場合は、おとりかえします。
定価はカバーに表示してあります。
©Kazuo Kobayashi, 2016. Printed in Japan
ISBN978-4-576-16168-6
http://www.futami.co.jp